Elements of Wisdom

By

Jeffrey Clark Lippman
B.Ed.Hons

To Stockings for doing so well with your Masters

Elements of Wisdom

Jeffrey Clark Lippman
B.Ed.Hons

Copyright 2010
All Rights Reserved
(First Edition)

ISBN: 978-1-4457-6969-1

I am flawed, limited and I do not pretend to have all the answers,

however,

I've been walking the earth for a fair few years now and I'd like to think that I've been paying attention.

I hope my insights are of some use to you.

The concepts I present in this volume I hold to be true.

Combined, they form a cognitive structure of a positive and I hope beneficial nature.

You may hold different views or you may agree with mine, as you wish.

Elements of Wisdom

Concepts of Life, Death and the Stuff In Between

Death is inevitable; it is pointless to fear it.

Life is as valuable as it is fragile.

Not choosing to live before you die is foolishness.

Foolish choices are never without consequences.

Balance is the enlightened path.

Decide who you want to be, compare yourself with that image; self awareness begins with understanding the difference.

To err in this life is an inevitability; to learn from your errors and become a better person is not.

Life is all about the choices we make, they define us both to our selves and to others.

Morality is a valuable commodity, it should be carefully cultivated.

Every time one walks away from ones moral centre it becomes harder to walk back to it.

Choosing to do wrong extends the boundaries of ones moral limits making it easier to become ever worse.

To abandon morality in order to save and preserve that which is of value in society is pointless, as once morality has been abandoned there is nothing of value left to save.

The function of morality is to benefit the individual, and by extension society, by guiding people towards good.

By definition that which causes harm is bad while that which prevents harm is good.

Our actions are the result of our choices.

All actions may contain elements of good and bad, it is wise to weigh the benefits against the consequences and be aware of the true cost of ones choices.

Strong emotion is like an ocean current, unchecked it washes away the self.

Anger distorts perspective, patience and calm restore it.

Compassion and mercy build inner strength and peace.

One cannot expect forgiveness unless one is willing to forgive.

A sense of humor releases stress and allows one to control anger, fear and upset.

It is unhealthy to take yourself too seriously; learning to laugh at yourself will make you a much happier person.

Be slow to take offence at humor directed towards you, affection, not harm may be intended.

Insults, derogatory language and gestures used with affection between friends and casual swearing in a moment of frustration are not intended to cause offence or harm, however,

intentions are not always understood and we should be mindful of the effect our behavior has on others.

Sometimes, doing the right thing can be so hard one is left feeling damaged and remorseful, at such times it is all too easy to imagine the wrong choice has been made.

Forgiving oneself can be harder than forgiving others.

Learning to forgive one self, in spite of ones past choices does not require one to be happy about those choices.

Undesirable consequences may be a source of sorrow and regret.

To apologize is to seek redemption.

A sincere apology stems from a genuine regret, regardless of original intention and is only of value if the one making the apology is willing to change and await forgiveness with patience.

When we believe we have been wronged it is all too easy to wrap ourselves in a cloak of righteous indignation and offence to insulate ourselves from further hurt.

Insulating ourselves from others risks rejecting remorse from those who have hurt us.

Accepting an apology allows others to grow and us to heal.

Courtesy and politeness stimulate good feelings and promote co-operation.

It is natural to want to be treated with dignity and respect, treating others in this way inclines them to respond in kind.

Speaking unkindly inclines the listener to become defensive, then they will either stop listening or become aggressive.

Behavior can be changed by motivating the individual.

Motivation stems from the need to either gain a benefit, avoid a consequence or better still, both.

Facing consequences and losing benefits are de-motivating.

Given a choice, people tend to choose motivating options over de-motivating ones.

Opinions are based on our perspective.

A narrow perspective limits the scope of ones understanding.

A broad perspective encompasses the views, thoughts and feelings of others.

Considering the views of others is reasonable, adopting them is optional.

Racism assumes the moral superiority of one group over another.

Moral superiority is a consequence of superior moral behavior, it is not derived from a particular bloodline.

Superior moral behavior is derived from a focus on ones own behavior and morality, not from deriding another group.

The right to defend oneself requires one to accept the responsibility of knowing how to.

To use force, or not, to achieve an end should be a choice.

To choose one must first have options.

Physical and mental preparation creates options.

As the body and mind are different yet connected, so too physical and mental strength are different yet connected.

Mental weakness can lead to physical overcompensation, physical weakness can lead to fear.

Physical strength can move obstacles mental strength can move hearts and souls.

Societies are made up of individuals working together for the mutual benefit of all.

To survive, a society must agree a set of rules and responsibilities by which it chooses to live.

Good societies respect, value and support the achievements of its citizens, while at the same time providing for the needs of its most vulnerable members.

Individual citizens within a society are represented and protected by their government.

Governments have the responsibility of insuring that the needs of the people are met.

Responsibility is the price we pay for the reward of rights and freedom within society.

The people and the government have a reciprocal responsibility to each other.

Government must collect taxes to enable it to meet its obligations to the people.

Inadequate taxation would prevent government from meeting its obligations.

Excessive taxation harms the very people it is meant to help.

The family is like a microcosm of society.

As government has a responsibility to the people, so parents have a comparable responsibility to their children.

Whether or not they intend to, as parents raise their children they instill in them values and beliefs, it is therefore prudent for parents to consider the example they are setting.

Any given family has access to a limited pool of resources.

Resources must be used with care and consideration if they are to meet the families' needs.

When resources are used to excess they are neither appreciated nor sustainable.

Over use of resources will in the end lead to unhappiness.

As an individual, one has responsibilities both to oneself and to others.

Responsibilities stem from needs, both physical and spiritual, which must be attended to in order to maintain well being.

Supporting and meeting the needs of those we care for is an act of love.

The greatest expression of love is self sacrifice.

Self sacrifices are more keenly felt by those who make them, then by those who benefit from them.

Accepting when ones acts of altruism go unrewarded with good grace may be the highest form of self sacrifice.

Love comes in many different flavours.

The flavour of love relates to its external manifestation and its internal intensity.

External manifestation should not be confused with internal intensity.

An appropriate manifestation of love yields the greatest rewards.

Over time love changes because over time we change, others change and the nature of our relationships change.

Change is going to happen, resist it and you risk destroying that which you seek to preserve, adapt to it and that which is of value may thrive and survive.

Love cannot be taken, it can only be given.

Unreciprocated love hurts, it can consume the self and lead to inappropriate feelings and behaviour.

When love is unreciprocated by those whom we cannot abandon, such as our children, one must be strong, patient and available.

When love is unreciprocated by those whom we must let go, such as an ex-lover, one must be strong, respectful and accepting.

People have a right to their feelings, and if one does not feel love then that is their right.

To have ones rights and feelings respected, one becomes morally obligated to respect the rights and feelings of others.

One should not expect love if one does not show love.

Love is a fundamental emotional need.

The desire to have ones needs met is a powerful instinct.

In seeking the fulfillment of ones needs, people will explore many options, from relationships to religion.

Throughout the history of the world people have embraced religion in one form or another.

All religions have five things in common, a creation myth, laws, ritual, an after death story and a greater sense of community.

It is reasonable to suppose that the five basic commonalties of all religions are basic human needs.

Truth is a concept.

There is no universal truth.

Our understanding of the concept of truth is dependent upon our axioms.

The illusion of universal truth is a result of most people sharing
similar axioms.

God represents the forces which have shaped and created our existence and the existence of the world around us.

The term 'God' assumes an intelligence and a plan behind those forces of creation and to an extent, some direct concern by those forces about us as individuals.

Belief in 'God' as an intelligent entity or not is a personal, emotional and intellectual internal debate of ones faith.

People have both an intellectual side and an emotional side to their being.

Internal conflict arises when our two sides respond differently to the same external stimuli.

Internal conflict is a source of stress and uncertainty and only by resolving our internal conflicts can we attain true self knowledge and inner harmony.

The desire to have more than one has is the desire to improve the quality of ones existence, however, the desire to have more than one needs runs the risk of entering the realms of greed.

How one responds to ones internal struggle with greed is a true test of character.

Understanding the motivation for forming a judgment is a crucial step in moving beyond bias.

To judge actions, be it ones own or anothers, one needs to consider the motives and circumstances behind the actions one is judging or there is

a danger of merely selectively reinforcing preconceptions.

Assuming oneself to be a better person differs from trying to be a better person in as much as trying implies one is at least making some sort of an effort.

In making the effort to improve oneself, one may travel many paths before being rewarded with success, but the rewards of self improvement can be deeply satisfying.

We set goals to give our lives meaning and direction.

As the circumstances of our lives change, so too can our goals change, there is no shame in finding a new path.

It is the pursuit of our goals, or not, that defines the nature of our existence far more than the goals do themselves.

Success is a blend of effort, persistence and focus, appropriately applied to a goal until that goal is achieved.

Until one achieves success there can be no certainty as to the outcome of ones endeavors.

Uncertainty can be a valuable ally if it is used to motivate one to try harder, or an enemy if it is allowed to

de-motivate one into a state of despair.

When goals fail to become successes two options present themselves, one can either abandon the goal for another, or a new strategy to achieve the goal can be formulated.

To pursue ones goals in the face of failure requires a strong sense of purpose, faith in ones choices and a degree of risk.

One must choose the degree of risk one is willing to take, balancing possible loss against possible gain.

In eliminating the risk of failure, we also eliminate the possibility of success.

A balanced approach, choosing the right risks to take is fundamental.

Through a process of contemplation, self-evaluation and introspection of thoughts, actions and motives, one can begin to understand one self.

With self knowledge an understanding of ones own potential and place in the world allows the individual to take control and chart a course through life.

Contemplation is a valuable tool, but is not an end in itself, if one losses sight of this fact and fails to appropriately apply their thoughts then they are in danger of achieving nothing.

To achieve ones full potential, time spent in contemplation should be balanced against time spent in the implementation and realization of objectives.

The number of opportunities available to us when we are younger often exceeds the number of opportunities available to us when we are older.

Opportunities should be seriously explored when they are available as they will not last indefinitely.

Missing an opportunity is often a greater source of regret than finding an opportunity taken was not what one had hoped for.

Not every opportunity is in our best interest, one must be selective.

As we get older we may still find opportunity if we continue to seek it, but we may need to work harder to achieve it.

At any age, education is the opportunity that creates opportunities.

Time is not on your side, nor is it against you, time just is.

The possibilities of the future become the fading memories of the past as soon as they become the happening of the moment.

The faster one rushes into the future, the sooner one is propelled into being the past.

Patience pays big dividends.

Attending to the needs and responsibilities of daily life, earning a living, raising children, contributing towards making society in some way a better place in which to live, both for ourselves and others is that which gives life meaning, regardless of where, when or how one chooses to live.

May your life be filled with meaning.